SIMPLE SOLUTIONS

Come, Sit, Stay

PLUS TRAINING TIPS

BY ARDEN MOORE

I-5
·PRESS·

A Division of I-5 Publishing, LLC
Irvine, CA

VP, Chief Content Officer: June Kikuchi
VP, Kennel Club Books: Andrew DePrisco
Production Supervisor: Jessica Jaensch
Production Coordinator: Leah Rosalez

Art Director: Brian Bengelsdorf
I-5 Press: Jennifer Calvert, Amy Deputato, Lindsay Hanks, Karen Julian, Elizabeth L. McCaughey, Roger Sipe, Jarelle S. Stein

The Library of Congress has cataloged the earlier edition as follows:
Moore, Arden.
  Come, sit, stay / by Arden Moore ; illustrations by Buck Jones.
    p. cm.— (Simple solutions)
ISBN-10: 1-931993-42-4 (softcover : alk. paper)
ISBN-13: 978-1-931993-42-5 (softcover : alk. paper)
1. Dogs—Training . I. Jones, Buck, ill. II. Title. III. Series: Simple solutions (Irvine, Calif.)

SF431.M818 2004
636.7'0887—dc22

                              2004003346

I-5 Press
A Division of I-5 Publishing, LLC
3 Burroughs, Irvine, California 92618

Printed and bound in the U.S.A.
15 14 13   5 6 7 8 9 10

Contents

Let's Get Started

If only we could wave a magic wand over every dog on this planet so that with one swish canines from all continents would automatically heed these three vital cues: come, sit, stay. There are many reasons why these three cues are so doggone vital. First and foremost, they can be lifesavers.

Say, for example, you have a dog who's determined to chase a squirrel into the street. If he had learned to heed the come cue, he would hit the brakes, stop, turn around and return safely to you after hearing you call "Come!" Also, if your dog learns the come cue, you'll never again have to coax, beg or chase your dog home. Simply say "Come!"

Dog owners love to show off their dogs, whether they're at home, in public or visiting friends. Secretly, they want their well-mannered dogs to earn compliments for good behavior from their friends, family and even the general public. For their part, the dogs unabashedly solicit head pats and treats.

Having a dog who understands these basic cues will do wonders for both of you. For instance, when the doorbell chimes and your dog bolts ahead of you to the front door, imagine the praise you both will receive when you simply ask your dog to sit, and he resists the urge to jump on your

SIMPLE SOLUTIONS

visitor. Instead, he quickly complies with your cue, allowing your guest to enter without being tackled.

When you are consistent with these cues and your dog learns to obey them, there's no longer any confusion as to who truly ranks as "top dog" in your household. Dogs understand and even appreciate hierarchy. They like to know exactly where they fit in the family ranking; and, it doesn't upset them if they realize they are ranked behind you. A clear pecking order is illustrated when you ask your dog to stay and he obediently stops in his tracks.

Mastering these three cues can act as a springboard for your dog. Because dogs are always eager to learn, they will feel confident about conquering new behavior cues and cool new tricks. Learning how to come, sit and stay lays a foundation for other actions your dog will perform willingly on cue, whether you hold a tasty treat in your hand, a dog-loving visitor awaits in anticipation or he simply wants to please you.

Throughout this book, you'll also find helpful training tips to use whether you're teaching your dog the basic cues of come, sit and stay or more complicated tricks. Training your dog should be fun, so be positive, be consistent and be patient, and you and your dog will thoroughly enjoy your training/bonding time.

SIMPLE SOLUTIONS

Nothing impresses visitors more than a well-mannered, obedient dog, so start training yours right away!

Come, Canine, Come

Some puppies excel at performing fancy tricks in front of a crowd. They can show their belly, perform a figure-eight maneuver between your legs, do a classic roll over and play dead, or retrieve a dropped writing pen. But, if your dog doesn't always return to your side when called, he needs to learn the come cue.

First, you have to learn how to outsmart your puppy. If you are a consistent leader, he will race toward you when you tell him to come, even when he's in mid pounce with a Jack Russell Terrier at the local dog park. Don't be dismayed if your puppy or newly adopted dog initially struggles with this command. Be persistent.

Training Tip

Ahem: attention, please! The only way to get your dog to comply with your training is to have her undivided attention. Dogs are easily distracted — just like children. When you begin any training session, pick a place and a time where distractions are minimal. When you're ready, say your dog's name, and wait for her eyes to meet yours. Clap your hands or whistle if you have to, and make sure she is watching and waiting for your cue to see what to do next.

Avoid using the come cue when you need to bathe your puppy or to scold him. "Come" should have positive associations.

Treat the come cue like it's magic. Resist the temptation to call your dog only to reprimand him for digging in the garden or chasing your cat. That will only make him associate "come" with a prelude to punishment or, at the very least, a signal that playtime and fun over. Each time your dog heeds your come cue, praise him so that he will associate compliance with positive feedback.

In teaching the come cue, prepare your dog to succeed by holding the initial lessons in locations where distractions are few. As your dog shows proficiency, gradually add distractions on purpose so that you can continue to remain the top attraction in your dog's mind. Whatever his learning level, there are many ways to teach the come cue.

Try a game called **Pass the Puppy**. Young puppies, especially, enjoy learning the come cue this way. With the aid of three or four friends, sit in a circle in a room or enclosed outdoor area. Make sure everyone in the group has a handful of small treats. Place your puppy in the middle of the circle. Start by calling your pup's name and asking him to come. Coax the puppy to you by holding a treat in your extended hand. When he scoots over, give him the treat and some praise. Then, have someone else in the circle call your puppy. Again, finish with a treat and praise. Keep your puppy guessing which person is calling for him so that he must pay attention. Eventually, he'll start associating the come cue with positive payoffs. Limit this game to five minutes or so, but repeat it daily.

SIMPLE SOLUTIONS

Use a positive tone when you lavish praise on your puppy for coming when called.

Training Tip

Be a leader, not a bully. Think back to your school days. Which kind of teacher did you respond to: the one who loaded up on the homework right before a holiday break and ridiculed students in class, or the one who guided the class gently and who took a special, motivating interest in the students? Dogs, to some extent, react to teaching much like humans do. Sure, most obey when orders are barked at them. But as your dog's teacher, you win her unconditional loyalty by being an effective leader who doesn't need to raise his voice or berate his pupil. Remember: Positive verbal feedback motivates a dog.

Another game that will teach your dog the come cue is **Out on a Line**. First, develop a reliable recall by fastening a long clothesline — about 40 feet — to your pup's collar. Make sure there aren't a lot of other dogs in the area to distract him. You should be in an enclosed outdoor area, such as a fenced backyard or a dog-friendly park. Let your dog sniff and explore ahead of you. Then, in an upbeat tone, say his name followed by the come cue as you reel him back with the clothesline. Your dog should turn to look at you and then head your way. When he comes to you, gently take his collar in hand, give him a treat without bending over, take a few strides side by side and then say, "OK, go play!" Then, loosen the line again. This technique encourages your

SIMPLE SOLUTIONS

dog to come back to you because he knows he isn't being reprimanded for some dastardly doggy misdeed, and party time does not end when he obeys. Never ask your dog to come to signal the end of your outing. Say another phrase, such as "let's go," so he will be responsive to the come cue.

To further strengthen the come cue, convert two classic children's games into dog-friendly favorites. The first one, **I Hide, You Seek**, is a fun and effective way to introduce the come cue to a puppy or a newly adopted dog who may lack basic obedience skills. The rules of this game are simple and easy to follow. First, practice the game inside your house with the help of a friend or family member. Have your friend hold on to your dog as you dash

into another room. Then, call your dog's name in a friendly upbeat voice and ask him to come. You may need to repeat his name a few times until he reaches you, and when he finds you praise him and give him a small treat. As you reward him, have your friend hide and call out your dog's name and ask him to come. Do this back and forth a few times and then call it quits for the day. Besides teaching the come cue, this fun game trains your dog to be persistent in his search for you — both are good skills in case the two of you get separated outdoors.

The second classic children's game that can be adapted for dogs is **Tag! You're It!** Start the game with your dog on a leash in an enclosed room or fenced yard. Call out "Tag! You're it!" as you lightly tap your dog on the back and run in the opposite direction. Let the leash trail behind your dog. Then, kneel down and deliver lots of praise when your dog turns and bounds your way or sits down in front of you. Repeat this a few times until he understands the rules of this game.

Now, remove the leash but stay in a confined area. Repeat the game a few more times. If your dog does not come your way, stop abruptly. With your back to your dog, bend over and pretend to study a blade of grass or some other object with great attentiveness. The idea is to get your dog to stop, come over to you and see what is calling your attention away from your game of chase. This is effective in the event you and your dog are out, and he breaks loose and begins to run away. Instead of chasing after him, simply yell "Tag! You're it!" and race in the opposite direction. This should entice your dog to immediately stop and follow you. In all games of chase, always have your dog chase you — never chase your dog.

SIMPLE SOLUTIONS

Training Tip

Consistency pays off. Decide on what verbal and physical cues you want to use for the cues of come, sit and stay. And then . . . stick with them! If you use the stay cue in one training session and then ask your dog not to move in the next, you will create confusion. Dogs learn at different rates, just as people do. For example, your dog may pick up your cues on the first day, while your neighbor's dog may take a few days or even a week. That's OK. If you are consistent with the cues, your dog will catch on eventually.

Turn training sessions into fun games for you and your canine friend; after all, it makes for great bonding time!

When teaching your dog the come cue, you need to make sure that he doesn't associate the word "come" with any negativity. If your dog associates come with being on the receiving end of your anger for misbehaving, you need to create a new verbal cue and then be certain to use positive reinforcement every time your dog obeys this new cue. Rather than telling your dog to come, you might try "here," "now" or even "bye." Whatever verbal cue you select, you must be consistent. Make sure other members of your household also convert to this new word.

Sitting Pretty

SIMPLE SOLUTIONS

The sit cue is integral to your dog's proficiency in matters of etiquette. People love being greeted by dogs, but no one really enjoys being knocked over by an exuberant Labrador Retriever or splattered with muddy paw prints by an enthusiastic Jack Russell Terrier. To a dog, there's nothing wrong with greeting a fellow canine by jumping up on him. Therefore, it's up to you to train your dog to greet your two-legged friends properly. Mastering the sit cue will certainly win your canine lots of compliments, an added bonus for you!

OK, let's look at some ways to get your dog to sit on cue. The first and easiest method is simply to catch your pup

Training Tip

Tone of voice counts.
When you teach your dog the three basic cues, make sure the tone of your voice is friendly, engaging and confident. If you are feeling frustrated or impatient during the training lesson, your dog will pick up those anxious emotions and the lesson will be a failure. Dogs don't need fancy college degrees to deduce our stress levels!

Use valuable rewards like treats to make learning the sit cue easier and faster.

in the act of sitting. The second he does so on his own, tell him he has performed a good sit. Praise him and give him a treat. (In fact, you should keep a few treats in your pocket so you can deliver the payoff each time he sits voluntarily.)

A common method to get your dog to sit on cue is called **Go with Gravity**. Consider this a hands-free method of training your dog to sit. No one really enjoys being forced physically into a position; your dog is no different. This method taps into the powers of gravity. With your dog in front of you — probably sporting a quizzical look because he has no idea what you plan to do next — take your right hand and slowly glide it up and over his head. Use a lot of animation in your voice as you tell him to sit. Your bedazzled dog should be following your hand as you guide it up and over his head toward his tail. This is where gravity comes into play. No dog — no matter the breed — can arch his head back to follow your hand without his rump hitting the floor. The moment it does, tell him "good sit," and heap on the praise. Repeat four or five times per session. In time, your dog should be able to fall into a sitting position with your hand signal and without the need for any vocal cues.

Another method is called **The Nose Knows**. Dogs are sniff masters; they have a nose for everything, from the scent of a rose to a chewed tennis ball hidden in thick groundcover. In fact, dogs can smell things more keenly and at greater distances than people can even dream of.

Training Tip

Stick with small-reward treats. Training time should be fun for your dog, and that's why using treats works so well. However, keep those tasty morsels smaller than your thumbnail; they should be small enough for your dog to bite once and swallow. By using small treats, you keep her attention on you — and that treat bag you're holding — rather than on chewing the treat.

Use your dog's super smelling ability to your advantage when reinforcing the sit cue. Select a high-quality treat your dog absolutely craves. (A tip: Use this treat only when you are training him to do something. It makes the treat even more appealing.) Hold this treat at the tip of your dog's nose and move it slightly up and back toward your dog's hind end so that he must lift his head up and follow it. This is an effective luring method. It gets your dog to follow the treat with his nose and plop his rear end down. As soon as he does, ask for a sit and then give him the treat. Repeat four or five times per session and always end on a successful sit response.

Some dogs can't help themselves. They just have to chase down a flung object and bring it back to you. If this

Training Tip

Keep lessons short. Dogs learn better in training segments that are 10 minutes or less (unless you have a truly attentive dog). You'll notice that after you begin, your dog's attention span will start to wane with each passing minute. Therefore, you should maximize the use of time during the first five minutes. These mini-training sessions actually work better because they fit easily into your busy schedule. For example, you can squeeze in a short training lesson before you head off to work in the morning or when you get home after a long day.

Training Tip

Think Las Vegas, baby! Slot machines, by design, do not deliver a payoff with each pull of the handle. If they did, Las Vegas' famous strip would be a bankrupt ghost town. Gamblers are attracted to slots because of the hope of hitting a jackpot. Psychologists call this "intermittent reinforcement." Apply this theory to canine training. Once you've taught your dog the basics, you can bolster compliance by offering a treat intermittently. Keep your dog guessing about when she'll be rewarded, and she'll work harder for that tasty jackpot.

sounds like your dog then use this behavior trait to teach and reinforce the sit cue by playing **A Fetching Way to Sit**. When you play a game of fetch — whether your dog is bounding after a tennis ball, Frisbee or other prized object — always incorporate the sit cue as part of the fun. Teach your fetch-happy canine that he must always bring back the object, drop it and sit in front of you before you toss it again — and again and again. Finally, give a cue to signal fetch time has ended, such as "game over." You can do this using a hand-sweeping motion similar to what a baseball umpire uses as a signal to indicate that a base run-ner is safe at home plate. You cross your hands in front of you and then open your arms wide. Then, immediately pick

The come cue could save your dog's life in case a dangerous situation arises while he is off leash.

up the toy and leave the area. This teaches your dog that you are "the wonderful keeper of the toys," the person who initiates and ends all games.

As a side bonus to this game, you never have to worry about your dog accidentally nipping your fingers when trying to wrestle the ball from you or getting into an unwanted game of keep-away with the ball in his mouth. Plus, it's a fun way to get him to sit.

Another way to spice up lesson time is **Canine Push-ups**. This fun game is anything but boring. As a bonus, your dog gets to ham it up and may not even realize you are honing his proficiency responding to the sit cue. With your dog facing you, place a tasty treat in your right hand. Move it close to your dog's nose to let him sniff it. Do not let him nibble at it. Lure his head back for a sit. When he does, move the treat straight down in front of his paws. His head will follow. Then, with the treat at floor level, move it away from your dog's front paws to force him to lie down. Think of these two moves as doing an "L" with a treat. Then, quickly repeat these steps so it appears as if your dog is doing a series of canine-style push-ups. Ask him to sit down, quickly in a happy voice (not like a Marine drill instructor) and watch your dog have fun performing. Don't forget to hand over the treat after a few successful "push-ups."

Don't forget to treat when your dog does a perfect push-up!

Staying Power

Now that your dog has mastered come and sit, it's time for the third essential cue: stay. Dogs want to be by our sides. If they had their way, they would shadow us at work, at home and even on dates or trips to the dentist.

The stay cue should be taught in baby steps, so you can build up trust and confidence in your canine and so he will learn that you don't plan on abandoning him.

Before you can begin the stay cue lesson, your dog must consistently heed the "watch me" cue because you need eye contact and complete attention from your dog when you issue the cue to stay in one place. It is easy to teach your dog this "watch me," especially when you have

Training Tip

Vary your locale. Your dog may be a picture of perfect obedience inside your living room, but acts like a canine Dennis the Menace at the dog park. Why? Your dog needs to learn these basic cues in all types of settings. This way, she will learn she must obey you no matter where she is. Once you have success in the confines of your home, gradually reinforce these cues with your dog in other settings.

Don't reward your puppy
when he half-way completes
a stay. A foot off the ground
means, "No treat for you!"

some delicious treats with you. First, address your dog by his name and tell him to watch you. Then, take a small piece of treat in your fingers and move it up toward the side of your eye. The goal is to get your dog's eyes to watch the treat move. As soon as your dog looks you in the eye, hand over the treat. Repeat a few times each day so that your dog will quickly learn that the watch me cue reaps some tasty dividends for complying. With the watch me cue under your belt, you can now teach stay.

Divide the stay cue into time, distance and distractions. Wait until your dog can stay on cue for a few seconds close to you in a quiet area before you extend the time, distance and distractions. Build on each success.

COME, SIT, STAY

With the stay cue, you must also incorporate the ever-important release cue, so your dog knows when it is OK to get up from that position. You can use a hand signal like raising your hand up with palms facing upward as you say "release" or "OK" or another word of your choosing. Just be consistent; always use the same word and hand signal to release your dog from the sit position.

Dogs — just like children — have short attention spans. Your mission with the stay cue is to gradually increase the length of time you want your dog to remain still in one place. Don't expect your dog to sit for more than a few seconds the first few times you tell him to stay. Be patient.

Start with the basics by getting your dog in a down position. Wait a second or two before you tell him he has performed a good stay. At the same time, use your hand in a motion like a traffic cop signaling a stop to oncoming cars. Then, reward with a treat.

Purposely delay his reward to teach him that you are requesting that he stay put. With each stay cue, you should gradually extend the time you reward a treat from two to five to 10 seconds and beyond. If your eager dog should get up and move before the designated time, do not give him a treat. Initially, aim for a stay that lasts 30 seconds to a minute in a quiet, calm place inside your home or in your backyard.

SIMPLE SOLUTIONS

Games make training more fun for you and your dog. In addition to mastering the basic cues, the bond between you will be stronger.

Once your dog consistently demonstrates he can stay put while you are an arm's reach away, you're ready to add the second key step in the stay cue lesson — increasing the space between you and your dog. Start by getting your dog to stay for 30 seconds or so while you're a foot or two away. Praise and reward. Then, take a few steps back and repeat the procedure. If your dog starts to get up, say "uh-uh" or another sound, look away and do not treat. Ask your dog to sit and try again. Your goal is to walk across the room or backyard with your dog in a sitting or down position. Once you are across the room, tell your dog to release and then ask him to come as your dog gets up and heads your way. Praise and treat.

Training Tip

Sound off. Clicker training — the use of a specific sound to signal to your dog that she made the right move — is based on positive reinforcement. Each time your dog does what is expected, she hears a click sound and knows that praise and/or a treat will soon to follow. If you want to use the clicker method to teach any cue, you have many sound-making options. You can purchase an inexpensive canine clicker at pet-supply stores, you can click a ballpoint pen, or you can make a clicking sound with your tongue against the roof of your mouth. The sound of the clicker indicates the end of the requested behavior and lets your dog know it is OK to get up. Timing is essential if you use the clicker method. You cannot wait even a few seconds after clicking to give your dog her reward. It must follow instantaneously.

If you already have a trained dog or dogs in the house, your puppy will learn quicker by watching them perform a cue.

Now that your dog has proven consistently that he can stay for up to a minute or more in your house or other place where you've controlled the environment, it's time for the final step of the stay cue lesson: getting your dog to comply when there are distractions. This is very important because your dog does not live in a bubble or in an environment that you can always control. Things happen — a stray cat suddenly appears on the sidewalk or a skateboarder whizzes by — and your dog wants to give chase. That's where the stay cue keeps him safely by your side.

Start with mild distractions, such as having a friend walk by as you tell your dog to stay. Then, have this friend walk by with a dog whom your dog knows and likes. Have

Training Tip

End positively. Prepare your dog for continued success by concluding a training lesson when your dog performs well. For example, if she sits four times in a row, stop the lesson and move on to something else.

someone bang on a pot or pan as you give a lesson. Go slowly and encourage your dog. Most of all, be patient. Remember: Deliver food treats and praise only when your dog ignores the increasingly tempting distractions.

The **Step on That Leash** game rewards your dog for basically doing nothing. Put a leash on him and have him sit or get into a down position by your side as you watch TV, work on your computer or engage in some other sedentary activity. Without your dog knowing, stash a handful of treats near your hand but out of his reach. When your dog stays put for 10 to 20 seconds, quietly bring a treat down to his nose and tell him he performed a good stay. If he leaps up for more, ignore him. Only reward when he is stationary for at least 10 seconds.

To help a rambunctious dog, subtly keep a foot on his leash so he cannot get up and move about. When he tries, he quickly realizes he can't move far. Wait until he lies down again for at least 10 seconds before you hand him a treat and praise him. Gradually increase the time between your praise and treats.

Let's Call It a Wrap

Once your dog is trained, you'll have the pleasure of letting him off leash on occasion, without worry and hassle.